The Long Holiday

Christian Kako

BookLand
press

Published by
BookLand Press Inc.
15 Allstate Parkway
Suite 600
Markham, Ontario L3R 5B4
www.booklandpress.com

Printed in Canada

Library and Archives Canada Cataloguing in Publication

Title: The long holiday / Christian Kako.
Names: Kako, Christian, author.
Identifiers: Canadiana (print) 20220404356 | Canadiana (ebook) 20220404372 | ISBN 9781772311693 (softcover) | ISBN 9781772311709 (EPUB)
Subjects: LCGFT: Poetry.
Classification: LCC PS8621.A4647 L66 2022 | DDC C811/.6—dc23

We acknowledge the support of the Government of Canada through the Canada Book Fund and the support of the Ontario Arts Council, an agency of the Government of Ontario. We also acknowledge the support of the Canada Council for the Arts.

The Long Holiday

Table of Contents

Meditations on Space Travel

It's all about the events, by the way—
meditation leaks, into the bucket.
so many things happen in the rain
average sewage,
ring around the neighbourhood.
living as me is like a big lie,
fake man landing,
fake takeoff too
glassing Iwo Jima sands.
second try on Fra Mauro,
last try on Frangelico.
breathe in, breathe out,
drink in and drunk out,
breath-alyze. deathalyze.
today I swear I looked up
and I saw the Eagle landed.

A customary disease.
My stem cells, incurable,
look for proof in organic chemistry—
amphiphilic, saturated by water
collapsible like zodiac.
I'm condemned like a building.
complicated concerns—
count my pills, count my votes
too much to tell in too many secrets,
and a falling apart sensation—at a loss.
Insufficiency of the limbs.
Made of thoughts like a siphonophore
a colony divided by self-realization.

And now of all things,
to want to be equal to my breathing.
Counting them, to make sense.
They tie the years, by coincidence.
It's not an effective return flight.
I'm not catering to the moon here.

someone shut me off sometime prewake
a long time in the air conditioned.
I looked for particulars,
I looked out of state.
I didn't believe anything back then,
an hour and everything latter day —
just a lord of the news.
in the prefecture of the Others,
everyone was after me.
now nobody gets it but the virus.
today in Wuhan city, Hubei province,
it's a novel coronavirus doing the rounds.
tomorrow someone else.
we're all just a grammar of germs.
hurry to the burrow,
the miracle of the mole, it's on me.
I want to meditate to forever, don't I,
without holding a sigh against it.
to continue living, to continue dying,
who doesn't, who didn't.

does this breath even matter?
not when it goes into that sky —
'scuse me, while I kiss the bucket.
ask for help. shelter in place.
return in doubt.
the sun is down with that.

coronaville, again, back to basics
it's feminine in French, like hurricanes,
with their super long fins.
can I be relaxed in expiration
borne out of another storm cell
the person that was ova
does this nose ever break
does this mouth even taste
put the cart before the happiness
and then, the advance of oxygen—
the carboniferous was a contest,
it was recorded in basalts;
I was over, overhead like cloud,
the line in the sand.
how will the children care?
no blame, no gain.
why don't you go for another silence—

people are personal.
the days of forget it.
enough pandoras as flew out.
and a load for pigeon movers.
the mind on the run.
look for it when most wanted
it's set at an angle,
the cerebellopontine.
craft of dismiss.
infections of individuals:
they all wanted it to 'go viral.'
viral videos, viral lives.
periods are perpetual.
it will come out of the air,
the former ether:
indivisible, unique as no other,

thousands per mote.
how far the blue —
going in one eye, out the other.
the injection world,
a study in sanitizer.
raging at the nucleic acids.
praying the mantis it's over,
pretend it's not there and never was.
how the world's off to a new start
a mushroom major, graduates of it —
intractable problems giving the all-clear.
there will be more deaths.
lost trail of crumbs out the forest
wolves of anthropovore
graves for accents.
over the way, planetary almost,
some new frisbee ring
no telescope ever saw.

in the end, play a few notes
perform for improbability.
relax, it's curtains.
those folds fall vertically —
children always used to play
hide and seek in them —
Bach is best, but I couldn't always sing
it's hard to understand...
to be mortified is helpful,
to throw up, and be empty:
it's the airfoil and it's the action
lifted up by the vacuum
pushing up on low pressure space.
it goes by flightdeck too
the window seat to save my place.

I have an ejection soul
idiopathic lightness of being
it is bearable — but only just:
the breathable suit,
the feasible boot
and in the end
it's all plane crashes on down
everyone gets that unlucky straw once.

meditate, lift your hind leg up.
beneath the snow, let it suck.
do you remember certainty?
spoof you every day.
but I wonder, when I'll be able to breathe out?
what is the mind when in the way.
I'm aching like the peonies
I'm never on time for the present.
I've never been strong, except by fault.
take comfort from the last surviving human.
it's a dialectic. and I'm specific.
shellfish once, four-limbed now
an order in the bath there.
the irony is to be here for the last time.
even my name is an absurd function of misprision
well understood in the past with, now,
just a continent-wide call for silence.

code blue or code blues?
it's the air traffic sound — a familiar sight
most arguably in the drip-drip:
type A bleeds well
cluster C never forgives
surfacing sometimes,
an X-Acto in the heart.
lying way over my head,

dealt the wrong hand.
the lotus works for a moment,
the weekend brings ships of pain
pray for me, I am in portwreck.
overall distraction is the daily achieve
wasted eyes are starboard here
can they help me to the bathroom,
I turned and missed the window.
too many curators, too many no shows
hospital greens, making the green one red
solitudinous seas in carnations
on the ground stage, cathedralic,
even in the free it's the breakevens
the no-never breakthroughs.
I have a couple of days a month,
the heart down the pants.
clarity is just lookalike,
it's the surgical place,
same old centennial syndrome —
the Gazans on the strip,
functionless analysis.
make a room before the exits
it's all the clap we care for.
it's sensitive to the x axis
because it's so close to zero.

the apocalyptic messages come through to me intensely
filling my head with buzzing
radio stations picking up all-nineties hits
it's the backbone versus the brain: a cage match.
my little patch of ground sinking quickly
now everyone has their own screen
facing the universe with a monitor —
absolutely the worst day came today

but it will pass too, worse will come.
in the old days there was the superpositioning beat
now we compete for who's most depressed
to be another Elvis is no surprise —
there is a new hospital called me.
the writer, with a limited choice of words —
the casualty function, down to the Fortean
the long-distance doctor, the un-son long ago
all the crying that fits the print.
back to the gritting of the teeth constructively
back to trying to disappear, surreptitiously.
space moves, advance warnings,
every meaningless causation down here,
I sink with the dismality of it.
later please protect me in amber.
it's a foolish world, I think we can all agree
too much liquid phase, too little atmosphere,
and then to think, the mortgage to outer space
we still owe in the atoms.
I was hurt by the asteroidal recoil —
and the everything backwards action nozzle.

Intelligence — ha, what is it good for?
absolutely nuttin.'
we'll lose the climate change battle
and larp a war instead.
they predicted AI would destroy us
and then they made it happen.
let them, so did the truth.
trust the transistors among us.
with the aid of anti-aircraft angels
indifference at its most utilitarian
it's never really more than hell.
'lower the stress boom,'

sudden cardiac arrest at the worst
wet birth and everything after
we turn in brothers and sons.
save all kindness for pre-Christmas sales
for the Sagittarians, it's Cancer now
carry on the work of screaming,
factory work of the domestic
fatigue for the Neolithic.
compact the Coronacene.
fold the heart, ask it for no more.
again, again, you wonder how much longer.
look at that psychotic in the distance
…no, it's your own father.
almighty plaster joint knife
for protospheric scrapings, finish —
stop that thought
wash that brain again

sadly their deaths are never in order:
'bite with the canines, chew with the wisdom teeth'
dumb luck would have an amaryllis come up
among all those saran organisms — wrong way.
an arm of glucose that reaches
then, inside a cardboard box:
heads this way, tails the other.
recyclage mortgage, flat, talk away
the death that doesn't care…
all advance directives coming out
all those chart summaries of the patient's thoughts —
filling the consults, so high, so flighty,
scan the ventilator winds.
all the worries never come except one
it's truer than it's ever been before.
I'm looking after these disasters,

and I'll never finish compiling
all our multiple possible apocalypses.
recording and reloading
looking for the good in every ascarid
I am neglected in the endless delay
I can go without mourning again
it will be the science fair never more unfair
upkeep of the adrenaline long overdue
the breath of all the missions:
do I really have to practice respiration hygiene?
all the tidal time, over the bound skin
outside the epistemectomy
the word loose, the clutter around the throat
an abrupt benzodiazepine, a cross in arms
the poor go back to the beginning.
if I come up right side up turn me around,
let me see the place where I once was.

when will it end?
when the other death-shoe drops?
when each of our breaths tolls the bell?
the dooms for another day-theorem
as it happened — news as last —
it just has to be.
a long day of nothing
and radioactive illumination
makes me see it clearly:
a boy dog of the earth, really.
the spit-farmer is ready — he lands.
fogbank was the codename of the filler
for the thermonuclear bombs,
and it sure was a good one.
it was once a bedside we came back.
time for the trivial now

a pandemic recommended exercise
of practice for death
and seeing things in wreck-licate.
it's ok to be tired
everybody is in danger now
bear the weather, we're getting closer.
save the last questions for children.
remember reading last November's apocalypse book?
happier days were, back then.
we're all for the insects now.
assholes crawling out from under the furniture.

if I die, will I do well?
brake all the way there
promise to do things right,
relax the paired premolars, finally.
it's panoramic, hanging from every error bar
mass mistakes, fatigue of illness,
English spoken only in fratricide.
the language has gone behind us now
it's luxury to be 20, wrong to be the 21st.
luckier in person for the aging
we talk, like humans, we source circulation,
children who buzz, sons of the lord of flies,
I have to be black and white again…
midazolam as deathrow meal,
sorry for the 19 at the end of your name…
I guess, if you're not afraid of dying,
your life is completely successful.
a major hole in the focus
the beeping of multifaceted alarms:
lines from your flat heart
and you cheated, by inhaling so deeply…
I have to work entirely out of my thorax now

to allow a lung not a graph
if I scream I will ask the atmosphere above
terrible tent, to make paper noses of us
with metal clips to hold them tight.
they call me crepe, crinkling under pressure
mere paper, set to with vocables
corrosion man older than he can,
a butterfly net in an effect.
some come in cradles, some come clean.
so long secondary infections
cedar works for repellant
the geometry is entirely conducive too
I'll coma my eyes, I'll wake up inside,
it will be currently over:
don't worry, it will all be just fine.
I mean, *you're over the rainbow.*

set in death
hard, bloody hard
integer to a rock:
everyone sings the blues.
the journey to the ground is long
all things lie
even the Columbian man.
the lambs evolve to be slaughtered.
enough consciousness to last
look down, it's a salt rerun.
the nerves in synapse
one each for the neuron of death
it dies in the smell.
smack in the middle of the brain.
all types are done.
something tree, do the lumber.
it starts with a cry,

ends at o'clock
a head that went light
like a balloon
like a window, from the top down
a fish's idea,
gaping filling the mouth
blunt needle said it all:
oh it hurts.

Poet With a Line Stuck Between His Teeth

Sitting here for now everything is ok
the demands of invertebracy
hauling the lungs back —
and water is light, too.
a sun that acts not alone, surprise,
a flower that was never part of a plant
nonetheless in a place in the air
half of a lifeform, perhaps,
petals equivocal, oddly,
genetic code replaced by poetic code.
solstitial reverend, happiness passed
is it right to catch those tiger swallowtails?
you always forget a smile until reminded.
as if it was original jungle, not sin.
wrong to be angry, wrong to be happy
onboarding the hospital bed soon
to lift the soul,
take that breath up for a ride.

Facile for it was easy
just sky shy,
like calculus derivatives
accelerations up,
thinking outside the head.
too close to summer, too early to die,
a number in the morning,
nothing by the noonday sun.
anywhere at home…
but here

to all those born unlucky:
may love give you grace.
it's your turn, around the planet.
people in place, in space,
and you rise above,
your speech to rain.
inside the water, it's day
a happy man returns, appreciated.
there's enough air in here
for the coming winter.
warmth from kindness.
for the love of one good woman
will save you.

in spring our thoughts return to vulvae
those tremulo-wiggly things, fir-treeline monses
vesuvial at times, in extremis,
subtropical, butterflies be-bedded...
the *ae* in gynae at utterly...
made for hover-dreams, for drama, really,
and they have names too, mouthfeel,
everything in green-shaved clean.
indelible in the hippocampus is the bead,
the hooded, dual-cruraed, double-bulbed
to bait vaginae in delictae, succinct in its
loose lips that sink a thousand ships
launched off sweet faces.
spacing ways, pentup angle in the crook
same pelvic nerve as memoirs
of areas tubed, topologically equivalent
to the coffee mug in holeness,
the donut, sugared, sprinkled, sneezed
in the calculus of zodiacs.
is it finger-counting in abacus —
that is elliptic to the hyperbolic curves,

perfect and full foldings, wet like
water equals life, climbing high
to the prime number tree?

Connect with light.
to be loved for it, once again.
To be there where you were.
A milieu in what it seems.
It takes a million to see one thing:
the heart can be full
full of everyone.
Many days of lost, then found.
It doesn't help to stand around.

do you know the ocean from the inside?
it's unrecognizable, perhaps by luck.
every day, saline revelations,
daily wash and rinse, surfs somehow,
but a wave is not a barrier, dear.
they are running out of ruins there,
fortune the fishwish and his cousin.
it's another form of tomorrow,
to pretend to be the canary
like the island, not the mine.
what do you think about when you think
of yourself? coming back in a hurry?
everyone should have a heart.
there's an effect of refugee, all over.
the morning comes early, these days
the end of summer is here
let the moment be wide and long
listen to the cicadas demonstrating for certainty
be on your best beach,
it's the poetry that knows, combined with Poipu
and the children are everything:

combing the impolite pelagic zones
cherry candid in the mouth
long meal appetizers may those be.
I want to be there for the smile.
review your location now,
red blotch conde-nast of the heart
minimum merman — pool-free.
everybody back, everybody back

all the language that made us strangers,
it sits there quietly,
part of the ever-increasing deficit.
it goes all over the world
a leg over the time zones
with all the words we could have said
that able dawnlight saving time.
a straight line it is, from the ordinary air,
tracks laid on silence.
stay before, stay over;
without the star and the start
the only cutout of the movie script
who could do the future for me?
the little crush that couldn't
maybe it was, maybe it wouldn't.
he thought he did, he said he would
but he didn't. and he shouldn't.
remember those shapes well:
the ear-shaped heart, heart-shaped space.
all life is hearsay,
sensate earthling, dropped here.
it's impossible to be at rest.
the heart is so forgiving of trespassers
when it should be chasing them off.
breathe my clay, cross my walk —

I'm over the hill, and far away…
it wasn't the suffering that stood me up
the snow so reckless outside,
years breaknecking along:
there was an accordion fold
and superpain brought me down.

the book of the moment is hard to write
I remember happiness like an old dream.
I have a diagnosis it's called me
the world changes every day,
sadly I stay the same.
there's trouble in nothing,
and it's available by prescription.
the intensity of art is sometimes unbearable
whatever happens next, stays next too
if I sleep I might be there.
always a fish out of water,
crossing several oceans by rowboat.
it was in a Heming way that we jumped:
now keep the coffins closed.
disabled infinity, how do I prepare;
late for the departure times, seatless,
myself in angular momentum
head caught between a rock and a hard skull.
in my world there are walls, impenetrable,
taking up too much room,
I'm greedy for kindness, a cat for attention
even the kids are too much like me —
too much to like me.
it brings me great sadness to announce —

there are too many funerals…
you can't demand kindness from people.
at most, ask not to be sucker-punched.

when you do just turn the other buttcheek.
let them go, dismiss them.
it's a latecomer world, picked over.
when I was 3 there was a pandemic too
it ended badly for the virion,
now everything must be precarious,
obsolescent, it will be our duty to be raining.
lost hopes, news worse than ever.
look through it all —
survival in a jar; it's day inside there
the smirk of the preservative
like a card-carrying conservative.
the deathrate of a smile.
lucky to be once loved —
best before birthdate
the pests are all indoors now.
lying for a laugh, like me,
being on the side of good, behind Plexiglas,
I can never be heard, just ignored
the philanthropist loner,
forty bones returned bent
the dislocated prayer, hands apart
friend to the dead
forever to the end

home at the other heart unknown —
plaid reason. doctrinaire air
it's like the local minima
pushing food through a small aperture
and all the pretentiousness off.
the grasp at straw law holds, always.
people will all be poor again
just turn it over, dear lines,
it's a life at a time,
survival by a cord
freeze the darkest matter

Over the pill and far away, here and back
a current cure, for now or nostalgia.
so much nastiness must still go on—
Camus says what?
existence stands alone.
to be an unactualized addict, fully faulty—
unrequited, unfulfilled, unfilled,
stopped like suffixal, grammatical in area,
stuffed, and clotting matters up
in the area under the curve, which is linens.
surfing the pharmacokinetics, as they say.
so many times, you came with me to work
placebo-Julian and a half in effect
in Dix-Hallpike dreams,
with Gulliverian tendons…
look at the long-range forecast—
it's me on the run, again
the ringed lifesaver on the river Ganges
the physician-proof fence.
they are stupid people,
they are dogs on the hollows of my heels…
every day a pill, priceless and perfect,
excipients on the dinner menu
and no one hears the corona-news anymore
there with the radiance and the radium
the cure and Curie, all over me
let it be 238 like uranium, fissile.
the hearing goes even, to appease the gods,
a stowaway in the ship of dreams
an example of recurrent fetus, again
escape from the planet of the tablet—the sequel.
can I lie down and you leave me alone?
do not resurrect, is the new order
—narrowly missing the clean-shaved messiah

for 15 years of good there was a wax museum
not Tussaud, Ripleys on the boardwalk.
I did the cone, I clutched the cosines
trigonometry of equals to me
to find that last patch of space
by the drunkard's walk of sobriety.
how was it helpful to be hopelessly dry?
now, go put your poetries in order

what pill will it be today?
the name of the holy ghost is one.
the imprint of an irrational number is another...
they call it e for existence.
some are ligaments, some are impediments,
some are tyrannical, some are crying:
and all in the name of the rock and roll.
the 1st is the vaccine, the second palliative.
concern for the children,
and everything in between.
bulletproof meds
locked and loaded for death.
each hole can take down a whole city.

I must've put all my sadness into you,
I'm sorry. It must've been on chromosome 2
just like the book of hours
my collected works all scattered and collated.
not just a ventricular defect
at the normal sixty sinus a minute
it's still my spirit the holy ghost missing
the father wherever you went before,
launched from summer to here.
when you come home
you'll be the prodigal as always:

where the ligaments attach to the bone
is the point of no return.
vacuum is for everybody.
oh god, where is that lachrymal vaccine?
when will your immunity be ready
moving slowly to nowhere
the surface of the heart — so round
such an ill meridian,
for you, from me…

will I cost you some?
that was all my fault too —
I gave you too much of me, blame me.
but you're not mine now, not ours,
not anyone but yours,
we can't go any further and
no one can climb the wall of your heart.
well, sometimes the sun…
radio-free waves, signal-boosted to home,
sent you light years, language without barriers
when we were visa carriers
and you got your way, always:
we were on the beach then,
one breath between the two of us
the fish so colourful and plentiful
don't ever say sorry,
the forgiveness is inexhaustible
take all you want from me,
when you make it work it lasts
and one day it'll be for life.
child in full view of the stellar nursery,
last cross of the Pleiades,
assume me already ocean-crossed

a severe case of anonymity here too
so it's disappointing to be human
bracket of lifeuppance
I swear they are free
I can jump into a big diet, like a hole
retreat me there,
frontline news worker
for Father's Day all the fishing worms
crawling up the hooks will be laid bare
it will be, frankly, at its best.
the absurdist apocalypse,
cliff climbing up the cognitive decline
just like in Despairville — the movie
'it's the winter of our incontinent'
living generic inside some taxonomy
may you have a lonely pharmacy too.
they come for the cards, stay for the plays:
family, in its sway and lonely, in between
and I'm everything, until I wasn't
as if it ever was the mother's fault
remember that attack rate for good, forever.
oh to be a circus clown again,
a life in other people's prayers,
strangers' prayers, in fact,
greatest hits of the 70s.

we had to coevolve
me and all the vaginal species
we learned to put it together
we built a hospital in a week, goddammit!
now a cold again, runny nose, runny eyes,
coryza and cohabit,
a congestant of substance —
we split the kids, let me leave,

let me have his smile, take the rest of his face.
everything will be lost
once I'm done with nirvana.
I mean look what happened to King Kong
subjected to the ending yet again
no, we learn by crushing Kleenex boxes.
they die for the monarchs in Mexico.
takes no time to burn those bridges
one match at a time —
it's a virus now storming the world,
here for the holidays again
billions of coughs everywhere.
it's the deep sneezing meditation.
they post the emoticon of soul
    ...you can smell his disease.
life is the crime, marriage is the weapon.
to share despair is the sacrifice we make.
free will in rigor mortis,
free speech in complaint
bend the sunlight through
so many negative terminals in this circuit
lead battery has to be drained...
a resonant quiet silence waveform
settling lower in amplitude
theft of sound in the air —
travels of the space farce
to go where no virion has gone before
it's the age of dopamine,
and it sucks everywhere.
aim the wireless up,
Aquarius is aquarium...

in a couple of days, bathe in endorphin
look up an epidermis or two
choose which one to follow —
son of a priest to come.
there will be lots of no love lost —
the moron pharmacist will be there
and you can be the farthest
from the entrance…
they predict a windfall for protozoans
and worms live in houses too
they suffer causes,
we have a contract with the mice
to make it to the year of the leech
without help,
put us down, be still,
breathe in, smell the chlorine.
the muscarinic is in there.
I put myself last, again
there were too many in front of me
others are better peckers.
it was all ending, anyways.
wish I could go back to that fishing hole.

People: Don't Take Them So Personally

In the end everyone has to disappoint me—
it's their way to say sorry.
even god must do it too.
more alone than ever before—
it's the forest for the dumbass trees.
loser of a billion ways
what do I do?
always in the middle of never,
it's my line, it's me.
the suffering takes many forms,
sometimes it's happiness.
the limits of time and space
the being there, or its absence
I'll have to meditate better,
do it in the grave
there at the end of the universe.
lay the marble down like the Tibetans
they put gold leaves on dragons.
but it's the year of the Geronimo Stilton
I think too much, I can't be hypothesized.
defeat of the emotional man.
Somalian famine in us all
a break in the bone of it.
is it the panzer division,
the sudden goodbye, the saddest, being final?
I'm looking for the flower, the lotus:
it keeps its head above the mud
and unwiped surfaces.
a baby listens to everything
the life in anything—
can you please be my -azepam

nitrogen ready, water in the tower.
get up and drain your testicles again
the lines are all so long on earth
I'm not an upstanding ape
look to the pharmacopeia —
a decongestant for the eyes —
another in your toolkit, we say
the prizefighter's jawclencher
sweat-stuffed pillow,
it's a hard life I was given
by the Humane Society.
look, my heart was not meant to travel space.

what would you tell me to do?
turn myself off —
stay calm, say it in earthworm
go back to being alone
grow back my own hair, be let go.
practice disappearance as the ozone.
attention deficit man — the new marvel hero —
amazing powers of hyperactivity:
what a great movie that would make.
emotional to the last exhaust
muffler with a chewing gum hole
so many lines, falling out,
on the deep end of the weeping.
once it was Angkor, all stone lions
now it's neoprene, and thongs.
I'm going to swallow a few more times:
it's the gulping meditation.
it serves frog well
I'll have to forget it and land clear
it's like methadone in Harlequin books
like 1, 2, 3, maybe 7,

all good assholes go to heaven.
it's not safe to be near
take it away, take it all away.
inappropriate man, again, doing what he can't,
doing what he garbage can.
nobody like him, and from Afghanistan on
it's always leave and dump,
like the redness in train station eyes
manual love, never automatic
negotiate a surrender with cardiology.
it makes the casino poor
a microcephalic man, like Zika
a duplex collecting system for the kidney
a diuretic it is, from the point of view of urinal
no peace for the mind, no rest for the heart
once set in motion like Newton
out to the Machian.
I want to, I want to in fact—
I'm born in forget it—
it's the rescue and the rehearse
lower the deaths guard, it's the grand old racist
come out with me, extinction:
it will tomorrow soon.
backwards to the Australopithecus
turn the backbone down.
getting filthy rich will make us stronger
one foot in the rift valley again.
hey that gun is backwards

what to do when the next depression comes to kill?
I have to line up those blisterpacks
three years collapsed like a folding chair
you heard me cry from Betelgeuse
how far I've travelled, inside my own mind

so many circumnavigations of the cosmos
those are the built-in blues
the once in a thousand years flood
if I take into account the seasons
there's florid psychosis too,
that backordered dream
that made holes in the soul
it's noon already, and the light is so dark
I kicked the tertiary bucket...
how can I be strong and so wrong
boxed and moving out of this week —
breathe in breathe out
tune in tune out

perfect entertainment —
down here, we see sociopaths are mandatory —
there too? never-ending endings, endless.
enable that bacterium...
Lysol will take our bodies away, too
cut the heart into thirds,
cut the head into sections — goldens, first tiers, etc.
thunderstorms are awkward.
decisions are made in back pockets.
wrists of failures, trials of palms,
fever knows best.
this is the age of crazy glue,
the ratio of rain to hydration, supportive care.
satellites of serious disorder
the art of the children, it is, to be.
can they be in the eye of the doldrums:
if only each cloud could breathe.
were the things of pulse for sure,
venetian at a loss,
it would be more than air.
old man, in the wind-shaped bed.

there are further places than the light—
witnesses all make their cases.
they tell me, it's free.
they interpret all the smiles for me.
I could've taken it down to a scowl
it's the cynic's pocket, I lined
the people don't know any worse.
he's a crossbreed between a liar and a jerk—
they happen everywhere, mega-where
but the disappointment is mutual, all mine,
all over stuck in the slaw.
nothing better than a hello, they say—
coming, and going, two worlds over,
the Olympic disillusions, it's checkout,
everyone you ever wanted to kill
but were too afraid to ask.
still, deaf dumb and worse
the unscrupulously righteous wrong us
nasty strong, carbon detriments...
crows everywhere, sitting on the electric lines
and the cover of down, the sewer cover
an existence that is army surplus
all black boot high shine.
it's like the correctional fluid for my sigh
from a deep breath out...

it helps to be lost in the neighbourhood.
we went from door to door like Diogenes
looking for one kind person
and, periodically, we were mugged.
it makes complete sense now:
so much is doglike to us, and wrong, to the dogs.
the great green fences that address this
they happen on every corner

even the neighbours are strays
counting on the long underpants home
the cynic can only do so much, in any case
our area is all full of fire hydrants.
they consider themselves social and such
with a deed on one dead end,
a claim to the title of top home comedian —
steps up to the hypocrite, the covets to every wife.
acres of asshole pollution fall
they accumulate at every territorial boundary
of course, our community is by far the worst
spread out in aerosols, microtubules pissed
their lovely herbicidal lawns, dedandelioned:
he ain't heavy, he's my morbidly obese brother.
is it a jack-drill, or a little girl shrieking?
kids that play with the cars, a disaster for sale
an up and coming divorce from reality,
an unusual system of disposal.
sanitation children, babysitter dumps,
the devil is in the details
just like hell is for others

you know that I believed I was an angel
maybe mounted on a pinhead —
it's called praying it forward,
and it rarely gets answered.
I'm looking for the cross in red, intestate,
anastomosed, beLittmanned;
disguised as undertaker in chief.
like Bertrand's set of all sets that don't set
I am that self-drainage ditch
words of the water loser, dripping off,
on the necklace of wisdom that chokes…
people are just plenty for us.

one hand tells me to stay soft, one to slap;
who am I to ever be right, you know?
let them all decide, kakistocratic as always,
ideals must come in clay at best,
or snowball strengths of grade —
you want me to be forgiving to all,
everyone, all of the time? really?
how much insufficiency can my valves bear?
how many other cheeks does my face have?
always jerk-ass and steady wins the race
just ask Achilles for his heel.
honestly the wings tear too easily,
Icaroid the moth that was Gabriel
who dropped his scales for light luminescence
falling with top self-defence compassion
on his proboscis trumpet.
he blamed his father, and the cheap wax,
he wasted away on the sunny road to heaven.
he worked too hard and burned out.
just blow it all into a bag, plastic clear,
leave out the sinus choruses, diaphragmatic in lift,
the whale spout channel up, uhf-style,
go where all the wrong memories stay.

in astronomy the weirdohole dorkstar gets out
crash landing every day;
mathematics fate closes in,
it's turn of the loser, the musical —
a queer for all seasons, maybe —
for you too, toilet pupil.
high school stays like an encapsulated spore
ready for more, your hair on alert
several nettles deep
whatever, way to go, surface ego planked

it's definitely not enough to be proud
it's definitely laughable to be artistic.
gay the plains on your face
the target on your duck back, dartboard bore.
I have been the lookout for the losers
learned the secret approaches well,
taught myself the invisibility serum magic trick
see-through skin yellow, go for icteral,
learned the nightmare of my own music.
the amused are missing from the jails
keep the cotton stalks alive
the white attack masochism blows,
words of the drainpipes, losses of stoves.
dummy misdiagnoses abound here
can you even hear the last breath?
more insulin, more reactivity,
you've engineered the emotionalese,
if you're hurt by insults, you're way too sensitive:
the mantra of the bully, and my brother.
learn to pay attention to them all day.
I mean where does the goodness go, indeed
everyone but me is citizen, coloured blameless.
…in cosmology, the black hole spins,
unwelcome is the singularity,
but the mandatory loudmouth is eternal.
school castes the first stone.

Schizoid In Schizoid Out

Like 13 years of Ezra, pound for pound
what do I do know, oh DSM-V
hungover from birth
when I step in the rivers of wrists,
never the same —
it's all flotation until someone's overboard.
all the evidence there's no heaven
you need is me,
dear god chlorpromazine.
go back to the cave, like Blake's Nebuchadnezzar
love me downclown
turn off the switch of the brain
turn down the nostrils flare
I'm a bullseye for what's called a pill.
but I can do placebos well.
cogito ergonomics, there's no crisis.
names of fools stick to walls.
of course, the mother is the protractor
in this serious pencil case —
now might be a good time to muscle twitch.
go sadways now, beyond hard or easy.
I can be nervous for a whole system
wasn't I better with less to write?
no, I always have to be thinking something stupid
(my father's favourite word)
all through the nothing new to say —
well, it's apocalypse aplenty now
fake news, April fools
this week there's no horoscope,
it's the end of the world.

to be depressed in exactly 2 months—
get it ready—the propofol, the potassium.
looking out, obey that layer of snow.

I respect catatonia.
Such huge savings in energy bills.
It was a dark and blighted ovum...
now I regret the days on over.
Since I stopped drinking, I suffer in silence
so motionless, and, I suspect, in a coma
like the mystery dark matter searched for
or the interstellar dust inside me already.
Psychology is so demeaning,
such sound and fury, sillifying everything,
so little to do with people, or anything.
Quiet for everyone, let them all speak
they know how to make the air move.
I became a great actor, following my doctorate:
learned to play well the role of MD
now the time comes near to stay fully still
quiet as the year of the mouse.
Long before the brain there was sleep.
2020 was a bad year, now it's twenty-twenty-won.
One year was like two, for all of you too.
But today is the first day of my breathing out
let it act as the troposphere
blankets everywhere in position
cells impossible to displace,
they are all wrong, those small droplets.
An art in insufficiency—headways collapse.
Moving only in the severe blue electromagnetic
and nothing falling on the spectra
black absorbs weight for the baggage,
the offer has been made, undemanded.

A madness suspect, a space in reality.
Register for Hell in time for next semester.
We have studies enough to prove it
the brown horse flies are correct.
Surfaces must remain dirty on the outside
things regenerate just as much as they stink.
I should have nothing left to say.
Could it be that mortality has really returned to us?
To make it safely to the past—
to die, following our own premature obit—
resting places that come in big boxy trucks—
I want to help myself too eventually
be my own pallbearer in white, in wings,
but I've shared myself enough
I have to finally let go.
Time to be forgiving of myself,
and my forthcoming end.
These are all the visions that are uncountable.
So long, wrong world.

is it any cold comfort to be Bayes?
to have been Robert on a scotia down
playing the not yet invented stats
at unfixed odds, living untheorized
with a 90% probability of life, & 95% certainty
then, to lose the game—the whole pot—
a gambler in coldcuts, *plus rien ne bouge…*
from the earliest embryonic escapees
of nonexistence, like us cellular combos
to the clever bluff of consciousness,
we are only alive on a bell curve, Poissoned,
with standard deviation of forelimb,
experts at regression to the mean-ness
pro-poker-faced in self-injury, operant…

zygotic nondevelopment, a common condition —
and chances are, we're High-Definition Dead,
we never even made it to the state of Nevada
unlucky survivalists of the unborn genocide
of undilated cries in the wilderness.
such are the statistics of pure metaphysics,
roulette for revolvers, wiped-down thoughts
in the shooting room, unsub cold cases
of stem cells, including completed abortions...
I read on oddsshark my current deathrate is 4%,
maybe less soon, discounted every day —
but luckily I was not a Bayesian by birth
I was spanked across the lap of the contingent
frankly Tylenol at the doomiest times
with arguments like supreme courts composing
about 18 lb carbon and less nitrogen:
a remote, unadjusted lifeform, interpreted frequentist.
but the home computers will be the better bet
their germanium switches superiorly antisocial,
rocking the numbers in a Las Vegas smoking zone —
knocking us out of the ballpark — Turing us out —
because there's a maximum occupancy
for this planetary morgue too.

it was quite a loss on Father's Day
like the ballad of one lung —
I couldn't talk, I swore and hung up the phone —
so Socratic, so hemlockian.
now the green algae return,
with the degree of block in the node of the heart —
a cursor in the clouds,
to boot me down and off.
every good family deserves a noise complaint.
ride it to amnesis,

myself equal and equivalent to an absent brother.
here's some pandemic poppies.
we find our purpose in spacesuit fashions
on the runway, titanium buttons, heatproofed,
waterproofed, vacuumsealed, transistorized.
we parents move by retrograde motion, like Mercury
like fuzzballs, to professional disorders, again
nerf-works, medieval guilt guilds.
thanks, now I can close the book on my kind.
she was the plaintiff, I was the complaint

you know, just like when you were a sperm?
blame me, blame the case itself
to be the disgust, the Augustine dysmorphic,
after another event of heartbreak
take the first case and can it
the licence to kneel on your knees
it's a long way back to Hell, isn't it?
to be all of the hospital at once,
from labour to trauma room,
from ambulance to morgue truck
I can't swallow the shame without choking
carbonara in the intent, really
mistakes are like blood, bleeding, bled
can I worm-proof myself now
hurt on the message out.
a problem in the air,
a mesocline unsuccessful.
I look at the situation reports
what a year, they say, this summer knows —
everything was from flying.
it was like a planet full of breaths up here —
the plane crashed and went back up —

come for the solitude, stay for the alone.
oh dear safety glide mechanism
be good, be necessary.
this little syringe goes all the way back,
costs a lot in property tax.
it's terrible for the social worker.
on the matters arterial there's silence
cells, parts of old organs,
lost hairs give me martyrdom cred
self-sacrifice is the luxury
keep the pain in the family —
they taught me self-abnegation.
stories tended towards enlightenment,
corrective mothers, who suffered closets.
meadows as the comforters —
roots are congruent down there.

you ate that smiley face, didn't you.
you fake emoticon.
you tried so hard to be a good man.
access is illusive.
some other seed, somewhere, grows
at least some bullets sell —
some walls fall.
let some soul out.
you OK'd that rope, didn't you?
you used some gas for mask.
the patients that made you who you are —
sodium born,
the win some, lose some life,
all away game,
every look now the other way
sadness is you,
all you alone

Covid-19, Hominid-0

Don't cry, it enters by your eye
uncle covid'll getcha
no birthday matters,
no plum surface landing.
no butterfly in effect here.
warm, come back home,
this is the worst spring ever.
hope for a cure for the sky.
the centrifuges keep us dizzy —
let's be honest with these mere mortals
respiration is all the news
it's D-day for the days, no?
tell us all about it.
it's the lungs, stupid
chambers to the uninvited
making up for the selling out of CO_2
from all the plants that just gave up —
does anyone need another way to die?
oxygen wizardry, better be warm.
all the words that's fit to footprint.
they remind you, you breathe
sometimes it's worth the full-on effort.
I wonder what's the immortality rate?
don't look me in the chart
and don't make eye contact too...

it's so far after midnight
we can work on the spring later.
we need to breathe better, like the dolphins:
they hold their breaths for suicide.

they beach themselves when they find a good one.
it was like I was in the iron lung
but it was liquid from the earth's core
revolving like my heart,
like the umbilicus that had the way out once
among magnetic drifts, making monochrome auroras
I really wanted to do it on purpose
with a mind set all through and through,
and I held it, swimming by the bends —
but I was unhypnotizable, just like I figured;
I quit breathing when I quit smoking.
look for that foster account for the kids,
be sorry for a week, who'd even know...
I had parents to blow me up like poolcraft
it's a weird world to be a person in:
pandemics anonymous — baby steps, baby breaths,
like the oldest human alive
nothing can lengthen, only shorten.
inhalation is the most irreducible case:
bilingual to the pulmonary, in fact,
complete housings, reiterated.
I can walk it all back to the other side
a man in the growth curve heading down
accountable to serum and to soul profits —
I, or an after-I, all on the way out.
but I can't pass into the underworld just yet:
there's too much lockdown there.

hydration in the demilitarized zone
anaesthesia in the glass half empty
clean up in galactic aisle 4
the year of the bat commences —
is death not a small price to pay?
so far, so discriminatory

that was the right time for life
open the fine tuning
no disturbances must come faster.
let me be the calm before the storm
an attack ways, in one angle
an aluminum crawl.
it's from the area piss there
the phasing transducer.
now from one face to another —
keep it on, keep it going —
forever like a fossil.
at least in the dark
I won't lose my vision

those documents were based on early lemmings.
the habits of depopulation
the rings of outer saturnian.
when your daddy dies, don't cry
it gets in by your eyes.
stay calm like the ocean for now
it blows over worn-out surfaces.
there are numbers behind the pain.
he's a regular, he breathes it out.
words that were sound,
waters that were tears.
however fit for the flowers
the mower that helps, the rest that quickens.
petals going over, I guess, everyone's heads,
the papers for the last ammonites
all on the bottom like the dredge:
nature performs earth hygiene again.
home for the workday, rat cheat,
in the carapace methinks
the spectre of Sartre,

a machine for Notre-Dames.
graves away; all the awfulness
is at our doorstep and now,
gravity just keeps getting stronger—
can I come home from this long holiday?

tomorrow the daylight—from saved to spent.
so how was that long-range forecast?
here the calm is the storm.
space, underscored.
original pandemic, a creature first
a thunder in the retelling.
more for every microbe:
some are conscious in dust storms
with rest stops inside winds,
towns of strangers, yellow perimeters,
flying picket fences of loneliness.
forms of enemies,
it was the me-demic, stupid
sick summer syndrome—
crown of thorned sweat.
now the turn of Mormon ants.
your card is invalid, bed,
a hallmark for the crying…
stop the terrorists of small talk—
fears of the sphere at rest,
there you can go steadily
dripping away, corona-clown.

I foresaw the future fail:
a curse on the dumb among us.
to pray is risky, it turned out.
news at nothing—I wonder for it.
stop at no one, call them back,

make them do it over.
the dog itself will be the spot-marker.
dropout neighbourhood kids.
look to termites for assistance.
it's the twins, the hemispheres;
the memory of respirations lost.
I put up with so much,
I put up with so small.
as in the razor clam retraction cut out the edits
tranquillize like a shot in the dark.
play man first, and me alone.
stay on me like a chin.
inside the scene of the crime
the temptation is to remain in the dark.
tomorrow I will not sleep

so long to the long-distance call
with Alpha Centauri, planet b.
the battery ran out.
if it smells like a dream, it looks like.
spilled milk everywhere, complaints come in.
it's the air we breathe, collects us in the end,
it gathers us up in husks...
the age of lost time falls on the nuclear age
'may I be excused'?
cellular certitude—no way.
with some tall, for antennae, considerations aside,
ask the ministry of chronic faults
to return with a pair of *pulmones,*
heavy sedation was once in use here.
proning multitudes may be best
seriously rotating, returning as the same
to somewhere in place.
you want trouble for a name,

a spot in the last home space.
the calm before the planets
a courtesy to physics —
mark it read, you're allowed —
protects the vastness of space.
the busy signal — the aphelion institutes,
dropped call ensues. solstitial support,
all those radio waves at the ready, gigaherzed,
all that we heard and all that we launched.
was it really an achievement,
those nuclear codes?

stay free, face
so much to smiles away
like a Disney for meridian
it's tomorrow, dummy
ever-moving averages
come for harm, stay from away
do we need the possibilities still?
we have all the endings we want.
if I could heal the truth —
but doctor, malpractice thyself.
a placebo concerns us all.
can an hour be slowed to a photo
I'm the clearest in the impersonal
a Buddhist trial is a draw.
the judge is aphasic.
I let a solar flare out of my heart.
the impossible lottery,
only the pool keeps me from sinking
at 4 o'clock everything turns off
thinking for months has done nothing for me.
tourist of hell, Pan-am Hades,
look on the flat side

the zona pellucida too
learn the lessons of cancers
how to carpent the coffins
I can make you all look silly
done, undone, look up to where —
roll someone in the carpet
hair of ice, coma what may.

letters, care of the lungs, never delivered…
though the escape from pulmonary is clear:
exit and entry, fully amphibious
among Pleistoscenic lakes and area moraines
fail together, symmetrically.
Carnot cycles are piston times pressure
that warm breeze is air times whisper
speech of the son the childhood dream.
attached in tiny pipes and throat-tied,
watermen for weeks spread white sheets
lost a whole sea in one wave,
swallowed the five vowels unrequited.
on the ceiling with weightlessness
at the aortic airlock, sub-spacestation,
save him from drowning with a plastic tube
a lifesaver on a nylon rope,
but be careful not to drown yourself.
where's the pill to keep him warm?
such Buddhists can lie still for so long
they slow a breath to a full stop.
the percent sheet, the lungs at a loss
sometimes deliver news like this
sitting on a weathered porch unread:
airmail — made of air.

practicing pilling, practice it —
a practiced rolling finger pins it:
that's an achievement — the Parkinson's point.
the palm behind, the metacarpals back
locked medicine cabinet as quarantine hotel
in the morning, coffee rockets loose moorings
you have interim logic, Boolean ideas.
fortuitous in the tidepool
you are coloured like cowry
you are five-abled like the starfish
like the scarab, rolling a ball away now
in a burrow for larval advancements
you see the cough approaching,
you hear the laughs receding
in the distance dopplered low
to the side, the no-turning-back highway sign.
somewhere in the cerebellum,
you start off for the long journey away
it's a complicated fetal position, at once Caesarean
and Brutean in you-too-ness
inside is the synthesized soul, purified,
expansionist like Alexander in the Indus
retractile like the sessile sand dollar.
you're in the cubicle and not fired
you are in suspense, guarded, rolled.
you are so far in between the thighs,
a restless relaxed, interior vein,
you feel the birth recoil,
like a lifelong reflex, long from one leg.
one fish, one Pacific:
that's the entire principle.
from the seamount to the sediment floor
you are crawling to the depths of freedom
down in the benthic zones...

oh wait, he's a first-timer — he's never died before —
deep pressure bends, air bubbles out
of your thick bituminous blood.
your muscles crack.

surface to air terror
death support,
do not suscitate, once.
refrigerate the trucks,
nothing not else
I can recall no more
at least, it's the same sun.
August and more, yet more
all the operational regrets, you know.
to return on a happy touristic kind of —
gravitational plan.
the age of percussion, palpation,
a word to the wheeze is —
it's all local, it's proton diameters
gestational mismanagement.

Letting the Lysol go, deeply,
diaphragmatically from the thoracic cavity.
Tussive in surprise, atomical.
Hydro-mental-codone is one teaspoon.
The poet in identity — unredeemed:
they call it irredentist, like Eritrea,
warring over red desert famines.
To be in isolation as a reflex, like Babinski.
The predictive fallacy off futures — sunk costs.
The long and sonorous cognitive.
For the strangelove casualty officer,
the case is getting clinical now:
Cough cough cough, Attila the virion

conquers the restricted airspaces,
globally positioned, like sputnik droplets,
aerosols generated in assonant rhymes:
I let a corona go out of my coronary.
Antarctica is for loners, glacier-ridden;
loser life deep below base.
Elsewhere, it's going really good for some
(bracket the happy) lifeforms
god-blessed, lucky lifesavers, flotillas
of organisms anonymous...

One day the new and proud white space force
led by billionaires for the millionaires,
will locate that extrasolar H_2O and
escape the torched black trillioned earth
(by then the Silicon Valley of the Kings
will have those failsafe immortality pills
fully anti-pandemic in effective potency.)
Because seas are there for sure, on some other
unmanned, unimooned exoplanet hiding;
they might be more wet, microbiologic, extravagant,
in those, humans will infect viruses instead,
give them transcendence, give them clarity
to go multicellular, their helpers, chaplains,
they'll live in perfect harmony, purified,
to first and forever do no *nocere,*
evolve symbiotically like corals' warm barriers,
asymptomatic like Children's End
their sessile cauliflower green brains
convenience-store super-sized to soccer-balls
churning out unified grand theorems and string theories,
proliferating with neurons and metaphysics
among the sharp mother spikes that nurse
wet hairs out of advanced ultra-intelligence:

comprehensive plastic surgery of being
all along the coronal sutures around cerebra,
chromosomal portmanteaus
to boost the unlikely humans to pure utopia
to become better terrestrials by infinity:
without hyperbole, with reality.
Saved by the messiah virus:
nails and resurrection,
crown of thorns of the soul.
Seeds of a brave new civilization:
infection is love, blessed death is hope.
Where we go one now, we go viral.
Come home, planet earth.
The kindness of strangers, forever.
Clap for carers tonight.
Bang your metal pots in the cold.
The snow falling dented today...

Saviour Masks

Today I forgot to breathe again
my jaw so sore from the perfect fit-test
strapped-on bad hearing,
running in speech-poor mode —
then, crisis hits — demonstrably
crime of the century's a recidivist.
new to the meds, as the fad world turns,
what is it, old barebones?
just a blue burqa-man pre-op
for registered major donor death
who forgot the last vent that bandaids:
an under Sunday yells fire!
warp drive, captain, let's get lost.
one more from space nine —
the old underdogs, the enterprise,
I fly past them too;
current for each lifewish
resuscitated thanks to wall socket.
post-polio, fare thee well —
put no shadow on the ground
just reach for the top.
keep me for last place,
Gautama may connect me later.
excuse me, I'm the big bore gauge
bandit-man in dark hairframe:
and I'm from the North,
the pearly life, lanechanger blues —
and I bring no hope.

is it come now? the time for tears?
masklines mark my face—
now older by N95 years.
wrinkles are decided in there.
ducts need cleaning
diagonally down from eye-angle:
you know it as Pythagoras, son.
and the masseter mm. of ECT—
square jawmaster nutcrack—
they put my hair in visions
all aboard Van De Graaff
horizontal frontal cracks that multiply,
sidewalk paths of least resistance
accurately predicting parabolic falls.
I am over those deep wrists.
the phase space of metaphor is vast—
sorry, can I help you?—
and muscles of the face are brave,
superpowered, atlas the dog-muzzle cup:
they keep me alive, don't they?
every day worries says the skin,
that lampshade makes acquaintance.
all the lenses in one tear:
microscopic for the stellar,
telescopic to a pore
they come eroding down.
salt in the wounds of the face.
you can't taste them,
you can't smell your own sweat.
do they ever help the earth
that spectroscopic water to recycle?
bear them with me, planetary soliton,
to turn to ice on rigor mortis,
splitting granite down to the chest.
follow me there, oh oxygen…

there are many actuarials — for real.
they cover every eventual: the quantum hesitant,
the cats half alive, the glasses half dead.
but lack of future is the prognosis.
breath of Windex, once, and I'm out:
one birthday, one doomsday,
be it said, this one candle was for everyone.
at the feverish frequency, long summed
take me home, hope for the helplessly helped
the one and the faithful death.
come from behind, leave for ahead.
there are many ways to destroy happiness
a terror at a time, a season at a sleep
the masks that print tattoos —
be the lookout for them.
icy comets, so sick of the dying.
The Rite of Winter —
I have come here alone to help
with a water bucket to haul to the next
with no one beside,
for those who don't even want it.
Icarus said, every battery drains
every silly putty wing decays…
helpful firsts stay in space
atomic numbers are frozen.
it's the periodic life — tables of admissions,
running of the Christian bulls
the takeaway boombust ecology
that favours intrinsic hollows
forgive them, they know not —
and I have my difficulty in rotations
floating on the causal ocean —
jettison, my sometimes wet cheek.
doubleplusungod may be there

showing up in person
as stocks of the heart crash.
it was in the spring that it started —
the beds tabled and lied
it will outlast the polypropylene
to good effect, downdream.
prone gravity, such a bad excuse
toeholds and concerned tiles
stretching the linoleum scratches.
just aluminum to can me.

every eleven knows
there is tick in the next bit
jaw clenched like marble St. Peters
teeth always at grind level,
then a quarried hole.
days of care —
written by blood, you know
how does happy walk away?
testing the sliding belt,
Pythagorean angles of fall.
dangle my drops of isopropyl sweat
at medicine hat, the sit slip,
curdle the cardiac death.
only two electrodes really matter —
mine and ground —
so far today fly Cygnus, to 1.

lost in the old hypochloric —
an H^+ alone, the water-burn —
the picture of disgrace.
remember me, oh alembic?
a hypothesis at rest.
silicon dioxide underfoot

for the step with plantar cramp,
St. Vitus is vital
stay on top of the gland, son
I feel sorry for the universe, really
every education is a roadblock
pick a piece of cirrus there
polydreams now —
calibrate the aliquots to awareness —
the goggles are on
but keep it below heart level
the soul extension device, believe it
recalipered to a new tong —
put it into chemistry, matchmakers
there, officials at the zoo
stop everything

is the air a trick
disappearing at your mouth:
the vanish in your body bit.
can you breathe your last now
and save some for later?
like untold lies,
I can see how masked I am not.
this is not a confidential disguise
this is no controversy
a grin underground is no joke.
is it a lie, keeping faith with flying birds?
how will it help those in need
the Montgolf features of it
vanishing away, in plastic exhaustion,
everything now falling off,
nothing but a cough for me?
bring it back for a high price.
pretend it's all atmosphere above

you believed it when you were born,
as a baby, and the angels cried Jesus.
all over the blue argon
they say today you're old —
white like white-out,
out of the fold and
into the mask —

shall I be honest?
my mask is my home and shelter.
my den, my cave, my hut,
my bower of collected string.
print new lines for this face —
those thumbs of cheek
will take them for criminology,
digits for down counts.
the best of the disguise,
big head strapped in tight
as vapours without climate
surface in overall dread.
heart-broker, someday-stacker,
a return breath could still go back
via chest-self-compressions
self-CPR mouthed to mouth
out of the black box,
augmented ego above the action.
heavy on the neutron bombardment,
I make the best of the day.
I make the least of my stay.
Holter the cardiac homework,
keep place, heart the humorist —
the aerosol is in there, take it,
warm like misspent kindness.
I still have energy to be gentle.

I owe my life to that mask
I just threw out in the garbage.
the cup run—runneth over my foot
it's the crunch of fishbone.
to the blind everyone's beautiful,
a mask will cover the frowns,
quiet parts of the throat again
make themselves heard—
with its taste of whatever-ene,
bring dream delivery days.
we deal with this thermometer now
weather we've had it cold or not
the cozy and the fit—
silently mouthing a wish for god
in the outer multiverse.
the nose clipped magic performance
and the grin disappearing again,
antimatter Cheshire, *eyes without a face*
got no human race —
but the return flight was cancelled,
with a boatful of no survivors,
only yellow lifejackets,
the oxygen masks come raining down
on my size M/L head.
I have been too rubberbanded in
to the Halloween way forward,
monster without costume,
to be alien without green
embryo before brain.

I'm in effect in every which way but here.
react the chain—in inner cloud
set it up for over the peace,
under the way

put it first like they all do.
now a cancer marks the spot.
people don't go forever —
they ride the earth into the ground.
comfort us with the night
and in that way
turn off the silence.

my mask is like gas
subliminal like monoxide
dull like this solstice
stuck like the first Soviet
baboon on the moon
six feet of lip across.
I smell the 3M
Dow chemical like upholster
Bunsen of the ur-helium —
an odour of the big bang.
noxious it knocks me
octane 87 like fallout
like an arson accelerant
no hose of Exxon in self-serve
or plastic blow-up poolfloat:
this Erie Canal dredge is all I have,
flame retardant all the way.
my mask is suffocant and sucker
lake lamprey faced,
a leech to the leech.
I smell the ice ages too
this urgent warm interglacial
layers by the millibar,
stuck weight of all sensations
on my adhesive parasitic
panic-attack contraption.

it's red on the main sequence,
several astronomical units lost
the deaf dumb and blind show
the silent, surprise goodbye
a last refugia and today
my only soloverse.

Happy Birthday, Coronacene

A flight risk presents itself in childhood with prodigals.
The balance of probabilities lies with the Libra
weights in the sky there hold us down.
So much of life is skirting the idiots.
They made me so drunk, before.
I'm a picky eater with these medications,
like with pillow placement, sleep sufficing:
sucks to grow old, sucks to see the old.
We're scraping the bottom of the future here.
Have you heard about the latest extinction?
Attempts are made on the wrongfully alive —
and the forecast is dumb like Twitter.
Guards of the joint sessions of mandible,
ignoble talk, ongoing war on the whales.
In nature they evolved to come later, the children.
what more do you need, after the birth?
the days are the thinnest currently, unfortunately.

Bad things always happen on my birthday —
the asshole returns, college complaints come in,
the years just get worse and worse, like perforations,
another Deccan Traps accords succession:
the complete saprophyte, volume three.
can it really be the work of decomposition,
the para-fungal legal aid again?
the earth of the matter is, I will be reduced.
organized Krebs cycle exhaustion sets in
and a consensus in chaos theory arrives
brushing the bandanna at my old beak
with annoying rock formations of imperfect cakes —
something in the area of red, and white.

the oops of the thing awful be bled.
collapsible hat of the celebrations,
will it be midnight saving time on that day
setting the permissions to draft beer?
every year since 1979 was a disgrace…
overall, the concerns of the late quaternary
remain incohesive: lowballs find peace,
tragedies unfold, like newly synthesized proteins,
and somehow the news is always misleading:
there are raccoons about, everywhere,
and there is very little hope, escape, or even post —
just a book written in illegible,
Northrup Grumman and fry in the sky.
sad days, bad days.

it's my fault it's my birthday.
existence inside nonexistence, that's all it is.
once the father, always the ghost.
depression is the concavity —
negatively curved saddle space
tending towards infinity
the earth falling all around
some stationary apple
providence is the sparrowhead buckshot
the blue blood of the horseshoe crab:
an extreme beach, waves-crashed,
last stop before suicide.
murders in self-reflection
your villainous superego,
tired will do well; the tera-lost.
and I thought my mother was there.
among the refrigerated trucks,
a planetary wind; children, go back.
there is math to the suffering.

birth was a reckless day, sometime ago,
sooner the death of 'what is death.'
it must come in a nuisance of tears.
hope I see me retire, my patients there,
wish I could tell them I loved them.
after I branch out of the childhood industry
turn me into a light and shade for trees
so much more than a green health card
alive with only self-referential dignity.
speech out of pocket, they all talk at once,
turnstiled, hot-nosed puppies with opposable paws.
alcohol was my pride and joy, my beer career,
it's no longer, I wish it was the end.
no longer no shorter.
no lung, no song.
perfect stories, story of nothing.
pasts of wrong precisions,
once it was useful to be a father.
a yellow line in time — but time to stop.
to die on Christmas Day
to live in the error bar
to be there for no one ever again.
poetry is no cure, it's only palliative.

I'm sorry. It took so long, but
I got addicted to the smell of the facemask.
full f-cked luck off, plenty surprised.
at least I found the fastest path
to pass by a million stars at most once.
travelling intergalactic salesman,
I got hurt by the sound of my voice,
I went broke by the waves of the air.
when my heart sank on a monitor
when the balloons went off

I had nothing else to know
I was torn down by the zodiac.
so no one could decostume me but tomogram
supply hell for all Halloween
wrong face at the hallucinations.
now I go everywhere for a smile
for a wink of mild peace
unless for a way to cheek with my face.
hotel manifold, remembering
the addicts' Phobos, and so long, blue.
laugh off a volatile while,
exhale down into an old rib now
breathe down into my finished chest
diastole untwinned — at once;
pray for the last to leave.
the ventilator at its word,
tells the supremacy high for all time —
born on the fire escape
fallen on the equinox again.
first rights on the moon
pity in the primitive way —
wet levels III,
damage the filtration plants,
you caught it, Achtung,
you got addicted

the aim of argon in a direction of air
sometimes it leaves a mark:
a prayer in the form of peace.
death to the way
plead it to the leader and deny,
deny the virus, carrot the root
a lawyer to the insane, intractable,
insurance of atmosphere and area

apples fall all over us
over the arch orbit, and mistake molecules
all in Brownian allegations...
noble assemblies, strategic karmas
sometimes potassium decays, like Palestine
breathing up an um
it's cynic like petrochemical
it's along like sods, isn't it.
you're an air breather, they say,
everywhere it makes sense but here.
you're propelled by doom, sure,
should be safe soon,
can I wonder next birthday too?
clay stool pigeons in the air
back to the black birdbeakmask
costume for us...

now the gritting of the teeth must begin
sour scream and a bitter bill
to swallow the savings,
gnash equilibrium offset
by a high surfactant dose of disinfect
spray it, wipe it, slosh it, swallow it
hit a hiccup on the way back up
pro skill in bruxism
some smashed phraseology
from an apnea souffle
the inside-out protagonists
secrets of Aztec internalization
remember, the appled afterbite,
the applied forgetting, heavenly outage
it's the agonic of the jaw, right
a burst temporal, a judicious
crown in the cavitary

Athena was born from that braincase too
it was murder on the meninges…
lame yawn, assembled compulsives
the Rome of collapses…
you are your own carnivore
autophagist in your image
area of *reductio ad nauseam.*
anti-metabolites accrue.
reclined in the shadow of the cheek
stay here and bite, dreametarian.

The Invention of a Solar System for Us All

And I was looking forward to the stay.
so it all comes down to the sound.
the crash and born on a space all of paper
and that hydrogen stuff.
can you flip over the tarp of the sky?
look to the latest galaxy, as example.
I must've assumed something went wrong.
but Andromeda steered off
their news was fake on transmission
and their deathday secure
10 million years ago with the light —
it was visible everywhere.
now it happens to us too
tabletop fusion in the cold —
today in our heart, in our cosmos tomorrow.
the thermostat set to low
infinity must happen again
living in the logic zone
losing it in the ozonosphere.
local minima regard me with sadness:
I was never a part of nothing, no
at the risk of space,
at no air pressure.
the lost gloves are off
look for the shooting:
old grave star

over the moon —
the stores closed.
stocks are low

sea of tranquility is all reruns
on stellar television, Aricebo and all
dismantled radio waves
and the courage to flag
and plant the flies.
the cavernous craters, intercept the calls
now running late for alien rendezvous.
in a quest for faces,
they search the homeless shelters—
successful should be the octopodal incursion.
on the moreover rover,
by the dock base, the population controls
fissures of second water
crack the tides down
falling backwards into still-outer space.
to give the gift of euthanasia—
his name the only suspect
one or the other in the spin
the black and white dust
we'll have free and empty parking
for all the coffins

a few broadcasts and they couldn't take it anymore.
the aliens went all the way off.
natural selection had helped them, in the end:
they evolved to their own extinctions,
survival of the fittest nihilists.
once gone it was quiet.
the key to life on Mars is the crosses
the moon is so over now
imagine the work of all those planets,
all of them vacated.
everything that was black was theirs
regression was that most mean

performed in deep absolute darkness.
but it will not be human.

if I ever evolve —
just remind me later —
it will be towards the light this time
no roots, no wood no food
no tripping over phosphate uptakes
no darkness for competition
just know a nectar from
the primary finalist colours
that put up shoots, in rain, by name.
let me select to manumit
so everything can be like Lent
purified like perfumes
with no leftover, no hangover,
no flyover or stopover
nothing remaining for me here
from the dirt of earth,
just straight into the light
without circling
without tumbling.

There are always so many offers from suicide to refuse —
sirens in the mist, Fossey forests…
Bridges called Icarus are everywhere.
I am still my worst friend
gone beyond child,
let the climate begin for the last breath.
You talk about self-harm
bury the phone calls like a trilobite,
a floundereye on things
in that puff of carbon dioxide, exist.
It took place as a trace fossil.
My brain is older than me

I write about age in pure porphyry
I am the last, the best argon.
There was a siphon that was a straw
volatile is the sky —
a sniff of the open soul, and that's it —
how do we know which spirit is ours?

subunits that ugly...
bearded week, road trip through Hades
several mental illnesses under the belt
I am alone now
American squid, unseated economy class
an Amazon in burn, baby
high stress string theory —
I am present today, only
put myself in my place...
abandoned hairs, everywhere in the world
and at a dog pant speak in tongues
equilibrista, turned off the vertigo
to hold mass murder in the pews
no I'm a diode to the end
breathed back to the occiput
toxoid lockjaw radiator.
become an all-dental life
decay to a lost tooth
down in the rift valley cradle.
impossible, impossible is this jaw.

blues in the river flow...
a taste of trauma care,
the white flag of winter
in the refractive errors of windows

spread by the dust.
services of the incarcerative supply,
all the freezing, and the still.
death, be not humble,
be not anything
it's the road not taken,
regrets in calumnious shades, sad,
all the cigarettes and
all the smoke so far gone...
needles now needless
syringes, that try out each day
harms of come this way
blues and 27, generation 'be' again
a sink in the drain that becomes you:
keeping it hid is the manly way.
it's only like being alone again.
everyone left to their own device.
a homeless guy in thoughts,
meteorite echoes,
the film that was this.
do not speak ill of the dead,
do not speak well:
they'll have their day
they'll have their say.

Epilogue

I'm sorry.
The long holiday is over.
This day is only today.
until now, it worked
between the lives and the deaths
and it will lose less than one second
over the history of the whole universe.
I just want to go home.
Over there will be my supergirl.
I lost my chance at redemption
I'm lucky to be still alive, I know.
Breathing the air hurts now.
One day this week in lockdown
she said her son died of alcohol:
now all those of us who are left
must stay together.
Say happy birthday again, someday later,
put on the sandals just like before
we must be realistic — it's all over now:
it was all just a fantasy
it was always just hopeless, all test tube,
the fabric of the universe was rayon.
But it gets worse —
future is all foregone
no 911, it's all alarm,
chest compressions are deep breathing
meditation is the siren
not everyone who is a lighthouse
can stay for these days…
No we didn't design the oceans,
they fall, divided

churches that are invisible now
fields of nightmares,
books of suns, the new manners.
People on another object, forgive them.
To burden us with their lives,
the mortality highs,
the life expectancy sales,
their reductions, their promo codes,
their bargains and all those new ads:
One more space species, spared.

I was a shift-worker in space-time.
so long, heartsuckers,
needseeker.